JUST A GLIMPSE

JUST A
GLIMPSE

JOHN ATKINSON

CREATION
HOUSE

JUST A GLIMPSE by John Atkinson
Published by Creation House
A Charisma Media Company
600 Rinehart Road
Lake Mary, Florida 32746
www.charismamedia.com

Publisher's Note: The views expressed in this book are not necessarily the views held by the publisher.

Design Director: Justin Evans
Cover design by Judy Wright

Library of Congress Cataloging-in-Publication Data:
2014910977
International Standard Book Number: 978-1-62136-782-6
E-book International Standard Book Number:
978-1-62136-783-3

First edition

14 15 16 17 18 — 987654321
Printed in the United States of America

Dedicated to my friend

"Little Tommy"

CONTENTS

FOREWORD

It seems every dedicated Christian has a great desire to fulfill God's will and accomplish something for eternity. Many of Christ's disciples spend their lives working for the Lord, not knowing if their labor has been in vain. We all want to see the fruit of our works, but God most times has us just walk by faith and not by sight.

This is the story of a man that wanted to become a famous preacher like the Apostle Paul or Billy Graham, but every effort to do so came to naught. Great ministers and evangelists get to see thousands come to the Lord, but most Christians seldom get to see the fruit of their labor and are left wondering, "Has it all been in vain?"

As a retired ordinary pastor, the author pled with God to just give him a glimpse of anything he had ever done that would count as everlasting fruit of his labors. This is that story.

Chapter One
THE BEGINNINGS

MY FIRST MEMORY of this world was as a very young child sometime in 1944. The loudest drone I ever heard caused my mother to grab me by the hand and rush with me outside the house. We looked up to see the sky darkened and a heavy roar that vibrated through the body. It was not thunderclouds blocking the sun, but an armada of hundreds of screaming fighter planes flying over—low, in tight formation. My mother with tears pouring down her cheeks hollered over the din, "Those are our country's finest boys going off to fight in this war! Many of them will be killed and will never be coming back again!"

I burst into tears at her words knowing that many of those pilots were going to die and not get to come back to their mommas and wives and families. Empathy for others was birthed in me at that traumatic moment, and the incident was burned into my memory forever.

I was born and raised by very patriotic religious Christian parents in the little southwestern town of Lordsburg, New Mexico. My next earliest memory from childhood was my dad telling me, as a little child, that today we were going to see the most powerful man in the world. Lordsburg was a main switching stop and repair depot for the great Southern Pacific Railroad, and President Harry Truman was going to do a campaign "whistle stop" in our little town. When the train stopped, the President of the United States stepped out onto a platform on the train caboose to greet people. My dad lifted me up on his shoulders and President Truman shook my hand and said, "What a fine boy!"

At that young age I felt like Elisha receiving the mantle of Elijah, and thought that God just passed greatness onto me! I believed from that moment on that I was "a fine boy," but I am not sure that my parents and others had the same sentiments.

They worked from 3:00 a.m. to 6:00 p.m. six days a week in their bakery and bread business. This did not allow much time for supervision of their children. We grew up as unruly kids without much discipline. Nevertheless, we were made to go to church every time the doors were open. There was Sunday school, Sunday morning service, Sunday evening service, and Wednesday evening prayer meeting. I am sure they felt that if they kept us in church enough it would act like a smallpox vaccination to keep us from catching bad behavior.

We were only one generation away from the Old West so we fancied ourselves as cowboys and Indians. Since Mom and Dad didn't mind us owning real guns, we loaded them with homemade blanks and reenacted our own gunfights at the OK Corral. I think our parents didn't mind us shooting blanks from real guns at each other because they thought it was safer than shooting BB guns and putting out somebody's eyes! In spite of permissive parents, God miraculously dragged all five of us kids through childhood alive, although several of us carried into adulthood wounds from our hunting knives, shotguns, rifles, and pistols.

Although not an angel in my relationship with my other siblings, I was protective and took a different stance if any outsiders bothered them. One worldly little boy with thick horn-rimmed glasses, electrified hair, and high water pants cinched around his chest, decided he wanted my sister for a girlfriend. He refused my warning about making advances on her, so we had to beat him up until he promised never to come around again! Without much parental intervention in our daily lives I felt God wanted me to be the protector of my younger brothers and sisters.

At times this older-brother-protection philosophy was frustrated by bullies who were bigger than me. One such heavyset older boy used to grab my brothers and me around our necks and rub his knuckles back and forth on our scalps until we screamed with pain! Because the boy's family was friends with my grandmother, she hired this heavyweight abuser to drive us out to her ranch and assist in chores that we were too hard for us to do. I think he got his "jollies" in life just by making us cry! We didn't dare tell our parents for fear of terrible revenge. Then one day he engaged in inappropriate behavior with my sister and there was nothing we could do about it. He was just too big. I felt God was holding me responsible to stop this terrible bully who intimidated everybody.

One time, at my grandmother's ranch, this oversized "porker" had some chores to do out at the corral. At last the time to deliver Israel from the Philistine giant's abuse had come. God reminded me of the story I had heard in Sunday school about the little boy, David, and the great giant Goliath. I realized that my middle name was David and with God's help I could save my brethren from this rotund boy-barrel. I didn't have a slingshot, but we had BB guns. We slipped quietly down to the corral and knelt by both gates. When he started to exit we shot him with those little stinging BB's. He ran squealing like a pig to the other exit and we opened up another volley! It was like being attacked by a swarm of wasps with no place to escape! That night we saw the red welts all over his body. None of us said a word about the Philistine incident, including boy Goliath. My grandmother, after close examination, thought he must have been getting the chicken pox. Needless to say, he never again bothered our sister or tried bullying us anymore.

Social scientists have pointed out that kids that are bullied sometimes engage in the same behaviors themselves. I am ashamed to say that my sister, one of my brothers, and I were cruel to some younger girls and their grandmother by regularly throwing rocks at them when they passed by our house. My mother happened to drive up in the car at the time, and I ran from the scene, allowing my younger siblings to take the punishment for all of us. Later in life, as an adult, God caused something to happen that would make me very ashamed, and I would have to apologize to the young ladies for our bad behavior toward them when we were children.

Early on within my young body there was a war waging between the Spirit of God and the spirit of this world. I didn't like to take advice from anybody because at my young age I thought that I knew more than everybody else. The spirit of rebellion within caused me to learn everything the hard way. Some of the lessons were so harsh that I still suffer from the effects to this day.

When I was ten years old polio was afflicting people everywhere. The Salk vaccine had not yet been invented. One of my friends was stricken so badly that he remained in an iron lung for the rest of his life. Another boy permanently lost use of one arm. My brothers and I went to my grandmother's ranch frequently in the summer. Mother made us promise not to swim in the filthy watering dirt tank where the cattle walked down into and drank. She said the polio virus was known to inhabit unsanitary places. However, it was so hot that I felt compelled to go for a swim in the slimy green water anyway. After all, nobody saw me, and my mother would never know. I forgot that God might be looking! On the last day of June—my tenth birthday—I was diagnosed with polio. It quickly paralyzed my body and left me in a fetal position struggling for life. In the hospital bed I cried out to Jesus and begged Him to forgive me for my sin. I promised that if He would let me live I would serve Him the rest of my life.

God heard my cry, and I began the slow recovery

process. I was put in Carrie Tingly Crippled Children's Hospital in Truth or Consequences, New Mexico. (The name of the town was quite ironic! I had to face the consequences for not being truthful!) Because of the distance from Lordsburg, my mother could only come once a month to visit me. She had four of my siblings to care for and a bakery to run. As a little boy of ten, I was so alone and scared that I cried myself to sleep every night. I sobbed, "Momma, momma, please don't leave me here alone! I am so afraid. I need you so badly. I don't want to go on living without you!"

The pain of loneliness in my heart and fear of new procedures was worse than the pain caused from the ravages of polio. After a long process of surgery, therapy, crutches and braces, I eventually walked again, but with deep scars on the inside as well as the outside. I was left with one leg smaller than the other. However, later it kept me from being drafted and going to war.

In the years that followed, my mother spoiled me because she felt so sorry about what I had been through all alone. This allowed me to work all kinds of things in my favor and to my detriment. Being the oldest of five children, I made all my brothers and sisters call me "King" and I ruled them like a dictator. When I did bad things, I made my siblings take the blame or lie for me. They lived in continual fear of what I would do if they didn't obey me.

I took up smoking, which brought great grief to my mother. She knew that I had wanted a beautiful Colt .22 pistol for a long time and she told me that if

I would quit smoking then she would buy it for me. I made a promise to her before the Lord that I would never smoke again. So, she got me the gun, but soon after I broke my promise and went back to smoking.

I took the pistol with me to my grandmother's ranch. Near the dirt cow tank where I had contacted polio five years earlier, the gun accidently fell out of my holster and fired. The hollow point bullet struck me in the buttock and lodged deep into my hip bone. (God gave me a harder spanking this time than I ever received from Daddy's belt!) The bullet caused the most excruciating pain I had ever experienced! The pain was so great that I just wanted to die and get some relief. I almost bled to death before they got me to the hospital in Lordsburg. Again, I prayed and asked God to forgive me of my sin, and again I promised Him I would be His minister to the world. The doctor gave me a spinal block and I was awake and felt everything. After two traumatic hours of surgery, the doctor that operated on me ended up having to leave the bullet in the bone because he could not get it out.

In the midst of all the pain and suffering, God brought a little humor to make me laugh hysterically. The doctor had such a large waist line that he had to wear suspenders. Bending over me with surgical instruments in both hands, his suspenders snapped and the doctor yelled out, "Quick nurse, grab my pants!" Before the nurse could react, his pants dropped to his ankles like a dead weight! What a sight he presented standing with both hands in the air only in his shorts from the waist down! Everyone burst into laughter as his nurse struggled to get them back up around his great middle!

Later the wound became infected, and the ten-inch scar had to be reopened to the bone and scraped clean again! Added to the polio, like Jacob in the Bible, it gave me a permanent limp for the rest of my life, to remind me that God takes promises seriously.

Chapter Two

THE VISION

As time went on, with one part of my life I read the Bible, memorized scriptures, and sang in the choir, while with the other part of my life I lived in worldly pleasures and criminal behavior. The Bible says you cannot serve two masters, but I was sure giving it a try. I was so stressed trying to live two opposite lives. It was like a person climbing over a barbwire fence stuck in the middle, unable to get either leg over to the other side, with a barb stuck in the crotch of his pants. I was actually relieved when the police finally apprehended me and brought charges against me for the crimes I had committed.

One night before the judge passed sentence on me, I climbed to the top of Pyramid Mountain, a peak south of Lordsburg. On that mountaintop I knelt and cried before the Lord. I felt such shame that I had repeatedly sinned, broken my promises, and let God and my family down. My sins had caused so much pain to my precious mother and all my family. Hot tears of repentance poured to the cold ground. I told God that I would not leave there until I heard from Him. I spent hours sobbing hard and pleading for the

Savior's mercy and forgiveness, knowing that I did not deserve it.

With no city lights, it seemed that I could just reach up and touch the brilliant stars of Heaven. Suddenly, without warning, swift-moving clouds raced across the skies covering all the stars from my view. Then a piece of the cloud moved from the middle of the dark canopy revealing the stars behind. The hole in the clouds morphed into a perfectly shaped heart framing the shiny stars behind. Then God spoke to me. His voice rang inside my head, "I am replacing your worldly heart with a heart full of the love of Christ."

Then the clouds moved again covering up almost half of the star-studded heart. What remained was a perfectly shaped fishhook. God spoke again and said, "I am going to make you a fisher of men with a heart for souls." Then He told me, "You will reach souls in your hometown of Lordsburg, and you will reach souls in Arizona, California, Oregon, Washington, Canada, Mexico, South America, Asia, and in the islands of the sea. You will also reach souls in the land of your mother's ancestors, Ireland, and in the land of your father's ancestors, England, and in the land of my son, Israel."

Then a strong wind came and quickly blew away the heavy cloud cover. I began to shake uncontrollably, not because of the cold, but because I had just had an encounter with the living God of Heaven! I felt like Jacob of the Bible when he had an encounter with God at Bethel. It was a long time before I could leave that Holy place. When I did leave, the light of the moon guided my footsteps all the way to the bottom of the mountain without tripping once. It was like an added assurance from Jehovah that he would guide my footsteps for the rest of my life. I never felt so secure or happy in all my days!

I decided then and there if the judge would allow it, I would go to Bible College and prepare myself for a lifetime of ministry.

The next day I related what had transpired to the court. I told of my desire to go to Pacific Bible Seminary in California and become a minister. Amazingly, the judge granted me probation instead of jail time, with the stipulation that I leave immediately for Bible College and not return to Lordsburg until after my probation was up at eighteen years of age.

I readily agreed, and left instantly! I left family, home, friends, and my old way of life.

Chapter Three

THE TRIALS

I WAS LONELY AT Bible college and missed my mother greatly. I didn't know anybody and it brought back the painful memories from my days as a boy in the hospital all alone and crying myself to sleep at night. I called my mother on the telephone continually, telling her that I could not make it alone and I had to come back home. She told me I had to stay, and I could not keep calling her. I was desperate for companionship. At seventeen I fell in love with a sixteen-year old girl still in high school who I pushed into agreeing to marry me. I was hopeful that she would cure my loneliness. The Bible college psychology professor said that our marriage would not work, an opinion based on batteries of tests given to us, along with much counseling. Our parents strongly objected as well, but in the end, both sets of parents, with reservations, finally signed the papers giving us permission to get married on the condition she finish her senior year of school.

After she graduated we both went to college, and it became necessary for us to get part-time jobs. I worked for a printing company near my college in Long Beach, California. At the time, John F. Kennedy was running for President of the United States, and they were holding the Democratic Convention in Los Angeles. The printing company I was working for was chosen to do the advertisement for the campaign. I made friends with Kennedy's friend "the Colonel" who was in charge of everything. God caused me to find favor with this man and he wanted me to meet JFK. We had a warm encounter, and the President-to-be had the Colonel give me box seat tickets near him at the L.A. Democratic Nomination Convention. He also signed a photo and thanked me for all of my support. I thanked him and told him, "I will truly pray for you, because I know that you will be elected as our next President of the United States."

After Kennedy was elected I wrote him a letter letting him know that I was still continuing to remember him and Jackie in my prayers. The President took time to write me back on White House stationary, thanking me for all my prayers and support.

After his election I was left with a strange feeling, realizing that now I had come into personal contact with two U.S. Presidents. I wondered if it was God's way of letting me know that He had great plans for my life. However, the way things were going certainly did not seem to bear that out.

When President Kennedy was assassinated I wept hard all that day. I hoped that he was saved and I hurt so badly for Jackie and his two children left behind without him. The letter he had written to me a few years earlier became really important to me then.

My wife and I had a very tumultuous relationship during those first early years. In spite of that, we were able to juggle giving birth to two daughters, adopting a baby girl, and adopting three pre-teen kids; all while working multiple jobs, going to college and doing evangelistic work. At the same time, our marriage was beginning to disintegrate and our finances were beginning to plummet.

We moved around a lot within Southern California, and I attended colleges in each town, adding to my education. I worked several part-time jobs while at the same time attending college classes and doing ministry work.

One job I took in Palm Springs, California, was as an office manager for Von's Grocery stores. At the time, former President Dwight D. Eisenhower and his wife Mamie used this particular store as their favorite place to grocery shop. We would open the store for them an hour before regular hours and allowed the Secret Service to check out the entire facility before they shopped. With nobody else in the place I had the joy of walking around with the former President and First Lady, lifting things they wanted from the shelves and depositing them into their shopping cart. It gave me a great opportunity to converse with them and share my testimony about Jesus as my Savior and deliverer. Knowing of their problems in retired life, I assured them that I would keep them in my prayers. They were a very reserved couple but their conversation showed that they really liked me. Mamie on one occasion said, "John, you have no idea how much we appreciate your prayers for us!"

Again that same strange feeling came over me

knowing that I had now come into personal contact with three U.S. Presidents. Was it God's assurance that He had great plans for my life? Still, my life bore out the opposite in the way things were going. I decided I was merely having delusions of grandeur.

My parents found out about our marital and financial troubles and invited us to move back to Lordsburg, New Mexico, and take over my father's bread business and wholesale food company. They felt that they could help bring some stability to our out of control lives. We made the move back, and it wasn't long until we were prospering financially with the money the businesses generated and our marriage seemed to improve a little bit.

The local Assemblies of God church was without a pastor, and I remembered my encounter with God on Pyramid Mountain. He had said, "You will reach souls in Lordsburg."

We accepted the offer to pastor the church, and God poured out His spirit mightily. A number of kids that I grew up with in Lordsburg came to the Assembly out of curiosity or just to heckle me, and ended up finding Jesus. The two girls that my sister and I had tormented as children came to the church. When they told me their names and how my sister and I used to throw rocks at them as children I felt incredible shame. I apologized to them profusely from the bottom of my heart and begged for their forgiveness. With tears they forgave my sister and me. I was able to use this occasion to explain how God forgives all of us of our terrible sins. They received Christ as their

Savior, and I had the joy of baptizing the two girls I had once cruelly mistreated as a child! They became staunch members of that church. One of my former high school teachers came with his family, and they all got saved and baptized! Many souls came to Christ during that time. What a joy it was to see God using us for His glory through the years in spite of our own messed-up lives!

With our new financial prosperity we expanded into a number of new businesses in order to provide employment for the many transients and needy people around the area. We bought service stations, restaurants, and a motel. We started contracting doing remodeling, roofing, and landscaping. Many of the vagrants that came to us for help found Christ, and we provided them with jobs, food, clothing, and housing.

One day, a teenage boy was hitchhiking near one of our businesses in Lordsburg. Our kids invited him to come into our Continental Bus Lines Restaurant and work. He was from the Island of Guam and had left his birth mom, a practicing witch. We took him home, fed him, shared the gospel, and gave him a room in our motel in which to stay. I had the incredible joy of leading him to the Lord and then baptizing him.

He then asked if I would consider adopting him and let him be my son. I said "yes" and took him to the courthouse to see our county judge.

The court agreed to his adoption. He became my son, and another part of my encounter with God was fulfilled; "you will reach souls from the Islands of the Sea."

It was amazing to see the joy that came into my

son's life and the desire that he had to share the good news about salvation in Jesus. One time we picked up a young man from Mexico who couldn't speak a word of English. We purchased him a Bible in Spanish and my new son, who could speak no Spanish himself, pointed to scriptures throughout the Spanish Bible and had the youth read them aloud. At last tears began to pour down the young Mexican lad's face, and he prayed in Spanish for forgiveness of his sins and asked Jesus to come into his heart! It is incredible to think of the power in the Word of God to bring a soul to Jesus without anybody but God's Holy Spirit to speak to him in his own language and draw that lost soul to the Savior!

Afterwards, another teenager was picked up on the freeway outside of Lordsburg. This boy was from El Salvador. His parents were political enemies that had been killed during the war in that country. He miraculously escaped and walked all the way across Mexico into the United States, ending up near our home in Lordsburg. The Holy Spirit led me to feed him and give him a place to stay. During the course of time I taught him English and shared the gospel with him. He readily accepted Christ as his Savior and I baptized him.

Then he asked if I would adopt him and let him be my son. I said "yes" and took him to our county courthouse to see the judge. The court agreed to his adoption after getting him cleared with Immigration. He became my third son and another part of the vision was fulfilled; "you will reach souls from South America."

However, my teenage son from South America could not get used to the American culture and wanted to go back to his relatives in San Salvador. I warned him of the dire consequences of such a decision. I told him that the same enemies that caused him to flee were still in power and could take his life. He decided he wanted to go anyway. I made him promise to write me and let me know that all was well. I never heard from him again. Only when I get to Heaven will I ever know what happened to my son from El Salvador.

Our older children all worked in our enterprises, and we home schooled them. The three older adopted children, as teenagers, rebelled against our strict rules and assigned work. Eventually, one by one they ran away and never came back. We don't know where they are to this day. Only when I get to heaven will I ever know what happened to them.

My parents never taught me how to handle money and eventually all of our businesses began to suffer from my financial ineptitude. I was teetering on financial ruin, and, to top it off, the government seized all my bank accounts, vehicles, and assets for years of unpaid payroll taxes. We never withheld anything from the pay given to the transients that worked for us and didn't know that tax was due on what we paid them. At the time we were feeding a lot of mouths every day in my house. There were over a dozen family members, waifs, and homeless people that ate every day at my table! Now, since the IRS seizure, I had no way left to provide for them. I could not get the Internal Revenue Service to agree to any type of repayment. The debt was too big and they wanted to auction off all my assets and pay it toward the overdue tax balance. In desperation I prayed, fasted, and cried unto the Lord, "I cannot let these children starve and end up on the street. I have nobody to turn to but you, Lord Jesus!"

The Holy Spirit directed me in penning a letter to the President of the United States explaining my dire situation, not really believing that he would ever even get it. But through that letter God showed that He still loved me in spite of all my failures and weak faith. President Richard Nixon wrote me back saying that he personally ordered the Internal Revenue Service to release all my bank accounts, property, vehicles, and assets, and also ordered them to work out a repayment plan according to what I felt was within my ability to repay!

Since I had no equity left in anything, the monthly amount that I proposed for repayment was so small that the IRS decided it wasn't enough to be worth their trouble so they just forgave the entire debt! I could never stop thanking and praising the Lord for His incredible mercy to me and my family!

I wrote President Nixon back thanking him for taking time out of his busy schedule to assist me with my problems. I told him that I would pray for him about all the problems he was facing while in office.

Again that same strange feeling came over me knowing that in my lifetime I had now come into contact with four U.S. presidents. Was it God's assurance that He had great plans for my life? I decided that it was just wishful thinking because my life continued to bear out the opposite in the way things were going. If God had plans for me I sure couldn't see them.

All my vehicles seized by the IRS had been locked up behind gates at the local U.S armory. They were returned and the padlocks were finally removed from our businesses, but irreparable harm had been done. Our enterprises failed to recover from weeks of being shut down by the abrupt government closure.

Chapter Four

THE VICTORIES

THE DOORS FOR staying in Lordsburg were rapidly closing. I remembered the vision: "You will reach souls in California."

My son from Guam had become very proficient at running our service stations in Lordsburg. We heard about a Texaco Gas station and garage available on Palm Canyon Boulevard in Palm Springs, California. We had no money left, but after spending much time in prayer we felt it was God's will to acquire that business. We told God that if he wanted us to get this station then He would have to do a miracle because we were left with nothing,

We called the owner and he agreed to make a loan with no down payment, carry the papers himself, and allow us to take over his business! Unknown to us the Holy Spirit had moved this man's heart so mightily that in addition to the free loan, he gave us all the garage's inventory, tools, tires, batteries, auto parts, and three underground storage tanks completely full of gasoline! With that kind of a start it became extremely successful.

The Lord led us to buy a home in Hemet, California, about an hour's drive from our Texaco Station in Palm Springs. I assisted a friend in San Jacinto in his

Assemblies of God church as its youth pastor. We attracted many teens to our services by advertising that if they came to our youth meetings they could take free exotic trips such as to Hawaii, and mission destinations like Mexico. This gave us an opportunity to share Christ with kids that would have never come to church otherwise.

A young Native American boy from the reservation came barefoot to our meetings. He had long black hair to his waist and refused to wear a shirt or shoes to church, much to the consternation of the congregation. I loved him anyway and shared the story of Jesus with him. He accepted Christ as his Savior. He then cut his hair and put on shoes and shirt without anybody telling him to do so. Later, I encouraged him to go to Bible college. He did so and went on to pastor one of the larger churches in the San Diego area.

It was nice to see one fruit of my labor, but with most of the other young people I eventually lost connection and have no idea what happened to them. Hopefully, one day I will know.

As God blessed our Texaco station and word got around about the exceptional service we offered, many well-known people began to come. The rich and famous, former U.S. presidents, and movie stars that had second homes in Palm Springs or that were just visiting came. My kids helped out on busy days. One day Elizabeth Taylor gave my daughter a twenty-five dollar tip for keeping the cleanest restroom she had ever seen! (Twenty-five dollars was a lot of money in the 1980s.)

My son regularly got to service the limousine of the famous entertainer Sammy Davis Jr. and used that time as an opportunity to share the gospel with him. One morning my son called me and asked if I would come down to the station and talk with Sammy Davis Jr. about religion. The singer believed in Judaism, and my son was having a tough time sharing Christ with him. I came in and the Holy Spirit gave me all the right words to say. Sammy knelt down on the cement floor, not caring that curious bystanders were looking on. He wept hard, pleading for Jesus to come into his heart! I never saw such relief come into a soul as when he felt the guilt of countless sins washed away and the flood of Christ's joy rushing into his heart. I gave him a Bible and had his name engraved on it. He was ecstatic!

We developed a close friendship with Sammy, and he wanted to continually do things for us and give us things. I refused his gifts, but one day a big semi-truck full of hay arrived as a gift for my daughter's horses boarded at a ranch in Hemet. We discovered that it was from Sammy and the load could not be returned. We were forced to accept his gift.

In the beginning Sammy was so excited about finding Jesus that he wanted to share the Lord with his friends. He couldn't get up the courage to share Jesus with his "Rat Pack" friends in Las Vegas and Hollywood, so he wanted to start with somebody he didn't know as well. He knew that Bob Hope and his wife had a habit of walking down Palm Canyon Boulevard at midnight after the stores were closed and the crowds were gone. After our Texaco station closed at night, we enjoyed doing the same thing. Often we ran into Bob and Mrs. Hope. So, one night he approached them and tried to tell Bob how Jesus had changed his life. Bob did not take him seriously and laughingly said, "Sammy, you had better leave the joke telling to me!"

That incident frustrated Sammy so much that he pleaded for me to go with him one more time and help him witness to another entertainer who just lived a few blocks from our Palm Springs station. I told him okay. His friend was Liberace. I knew Liberace was a great pianist, but I was ignorant about his lifestyle. When we arrived there were a number of Rolls Royces in the driveway at the rear of the house, with loud music coming from the open back door. Sammy had me follow him in through the open door without knocking. I was shocked to see the party was all men with some of them in swimsuits drinking and kissing each other. Some were lying on top of a grand piano, while others were lying on the sofas petting each other.

Liberace hollered, "Hey Sammy, welcome to my party!"

Sammy responded, "Hi Lib, I want you to meet my pastor, John Atkinson."

Liberace, obviously intoxicated, started laughing hysterically and replied, "Oh Sammy, that's a good one! The friend you brought to our party is your pastor? Good one! That's a classic!"

Then the other men broke into laughter as well. Sammy's dark face flushed with anger. Then he grabbed me by the arm and said, "Pastor John, we are getting out of here." Then he yelled, "Lib, you will just have to go to hell! We aren't staying in this nasty place any longer!"

That was the last time Sammy asked me to help him in sharing the gospel with his friends.

One New Year's, Sammy chartered a big bus and took about thirty young people from our church youth group to the Rose Bowl parade in Pasadena, California. He sang on the bus and entertained the kids the entire way. Before the parade, Sammy and his wife treated us all to a home-cooked breakfast of ham, eggs and hotcakes at an old family home he owned right on the parade route. We all got to watch the Rose Bowl parade from his front yard sitting in Sammy's lawn chairs!

One time Sammy decided to visit our church. I made all the people promise in advance not to take his picture or ask for his autograph. "Just treat him like any other brother in the Lord," I admonished.

Everybody promised that they would do so, but on the Sunday that Sammy Davis Jr. came to church, the people broke that promise. After the service I saw cameras flashing and people with pens and paper held out asking for his autograph! Sammy desperately wanted to be treated like anybody else at church so he felt he could not return again.

We tried to keep his conversion a secret but word leaked out after he visited our church. Soon Trinity Broadcasting Network (TBN) contacted me and wanted me to bring Sammy Davis Jr. for a television interview. Sammy declined and told me, "I don't want to bring reproach on my Lord. I confess, I still haven't got victory over drinking and smoking. That would make me look like a hypocrite."

Sammy knew about how important I felt his example was to kids and how important it was to change his image. One time he called me weeping profusely. He was in Japan and told me that he had just finished making a Japanese beer commercial because he needed the money. He felt so ashamed that he let Jesus down, and he decided that he had destroyed any chance of being a role model to kids. I prayed for him until he felt God's forgiveness and cleansing. We both felt Jesus had freed him totally from those habits.

When Sammy would fly back to Palm Springs after filming or entertaining, often he would call and see if I was in town and if so ask me to pick him up at the airport. On one occasion after meeting his plane I took him to his condo and carried his suitcase into the bedroom. He yelled from the kitchen just to throw it on the bed. When I did so, the clasps on the overstuffed suitcase popped open exposing a bottle of liquor. I quickly wrote a little note that said, *"THIS IS A NO-NO!"Signed: "GOD".*

I placed the message on the bottle and reclosed the suitcase. I would have loved to have been a fly on the wall and seen Sammy's face when he opened that case! However, he never said a word to me about it. I wonder if he really thought that the note was from God!

After a while Sammy started calling me repeatedly

crying, "Pastor, please pray for me, I have fallen off the wagon again."

I prayed for him each time he called. We stayed in touch until shortly before his death. I could not understand why he could not get victory over his addictions. I know he loved the Lord. His death wounded me deeply. I hope and pray to see my old friend in heaven someday.

The San Jacinto Assembly of God decided to help us start our own church in neighboring Hemet, where we lived. Like in my vision received as a teenager, my heart burned to please God, and I had an insatiable desire to get as many people saved as I could. God anointed me with power, and the Holy Spirit gave me the words to reach some of the most unreachable people. As a young teen, one of my daughters received a similar anointing and hunger for souls. We went into the ghettos together, and she operated a puppet stage and played the accordion to draw crowds while I preached. Kids, moms, and dads came to Christ. At the same time on the other side of the mountain in Palm Springs, my son was witnessing and praying with people to accept Christ right in the Texaco station garage!

God continued to prosper our business, and we opened another Texaco station and garage in San Bernardino, California. My son ran back and forth between there and Palm Springs to manage them. By this time our eldest daughter was a teenager and able to help out, when not attending our newly established Christian school.

During this same period God gave me a special anointing to pray for the sick. Astonishing miracles began to happen when I prayed. One Sunday over a dozen seriously ill people came forward in church for prayer. I prayed over them and declared by the Holy Spirit that they were all healed. I instructed them to go to their doctors and be examined. The next week all came back declaring that a miracle had taken place and they were totally healed!

When I visited people at the hospital and prayed for them, many were healed and left their hospital beds. One sinful man in a deep coma dying of liver disease from excessive drinking was on a respirator and declared to be brain-dead by the doctor. They encouraged his wife to allow them to pull the plug and let him die. She pleaded for me to come pray for him. I went into the intensive care ward of the hospital and laid my hands on his chest and commanded him to get up out of bed. Nothing happened. I prayed again with tears and pleas for God to save him. I even read scriptures about salvation and healing to his comatose body. Still nothing happened. Finally, feeling very discouraged I went home. When I got there the phone rang. It was the man's hysterical wife calling. I knew he must have died. She was stuttering loudly, "Pastor, when you left the intensive care, my husband woke up, pulled the tubes out of his arms, put on his clothes and made me take him home!"

I went to their house, and there he was, kneeling and praying to Jesus, wanting forgiveness and salvation! He said that he had heard everything I told him while in the coma! God had miraculously healed him and brought him back from his deathbed!

Great revival broke out when this news got around. Many more were saved and healed.

A friend of mine personally knew the great singer and acclaimed father of rock 'n' roll, Little Richard. I heard that he had recently gotten saved, and so I invited him to our church for a concert and to give his testimony. He agreed to do it, so I met with him and asked him if he had truly given up his old life-style. I wanted to be sure, since my experience with Sammy Davis Jr. was still fresh in my mind. Little Richard assured me that he had completely given up his old way of life. I asked him, "Are you still walking one hundred percent with Jesus?"

He answered me back, "Is the Pope still one hundred percent Catholic?"

Little Richard was a real drawing card to our church, and we had the largest crowds in our history attend. Besides his Gospel songs, we decided to allow him to fill in with some of his signature rock songs (an unorthodox thing to do in a church!) and give his testimony on how Jesus had cleaned up his life and saved his soul. I followed it with a short gospel message and many people came forward to accept Christ as their Savior.

Thus the vision from God was being fulfilled: "You shall reach souls in California."

Chapter Five

THE DESTRUCTION

I WAS VERY PROUD about all that I had accomplished in such a short time. The only thing that wasn't a short time was finally receiving my doctoral degree in theology. By the time I received it, I had been going to one school or another nonstop since I was six years of age! That was almost forty years of my life! I think that would qualify a person to be labeled as a "professional student."

I loved to give success reports at our district ministers' meetings. I pitied other pastors that were not experiencing the same move of God in their churches.

I didn't realize it at the time, but my pride was a terrible sin against God that He would have to correct. That sin was going to cause me and my family to have a great fall. I did not even know that the gift of healing was withdrawn. I did not realize that the faucets of financial blessings had been turned off. I did not recognize that God's canopy of protection over my family had been broken. I was blinded and could not see that I, my wife, my son, and my daughters were all drifting into bad situations.

One late night robbers held up my eldest daughter, who was running our Texaco Station in San Bernardino while my son was working at the station on the other side of the city. One of the gunmen took her into the back room and told her, "Kneel down and say your final prayers, and then I am going to shoot you in the head."

She obeyed him and cried out to the Lord in prayer, and somehow the Spirit of God prevented the criminal from taking her life. We still do not know how God intervened, but the robbers decided not to kill her. Instead, they just tied her up in the back room and then loaded up all our tools, money and merchandise into a truck and sped away.

At closing time, my son returned and found my daughter tied up. When he called me, I was horrified at what had happened! I wept and thanked God for sparing my daughter's life in spite of my foolishness of allowing a teenage girl to operate a service station alone at night. We closed the station and pulled our businesses out of San Bernardino.

I still had never learned money management, and eventually our Texaco station in Palm Springs went broke. We had to close it up and let the property go back to the original owner. My financial acumen was no better in the church. We had grown so fast that we had to go to multiple services on Sundays in order to accommodate all the people that were coming. We hastily entered into a building program with an inexperienced contractor that caused us to lose all the money we had borrowed for the land and building. We ended up losing the church building, the school, and the land for the new building. We were forced to go into a small rented facility to try and keep things going, but everything went downhill from there.

In spite of all the financial woes, the church raised money to send me to Israel. A friend said that he could book us meetings if I would come with him. I thought that at last God was going to fulfill the part of the vision He gave me about reaching souls in Israel.

During this same time our church treasurer's grandson became gravely ill with an enlarged heart and was taken to UCLA Medical Center in Los Angeles. I felt that it was very important that I be with the boy at the hospital, so I canceled my trip to Israel and stayed at a hotel near the hospital in Los Angeles. This way I could be with the young man on a daily basis until God touched him. I fully expected God to heal the boy after I prayed fervently because most everybody in the past that I prayed for God had healed. I became alarmed when the boy's condition worsened, so I stayed on and prayed all the more.

One day I saw a young woman weeping in the hospital waiting room. I went over and introduced myself and asked her what was the matter. She told me that her name was Kathy and that her little boy, Tommy, was in the hospital dying of cancer. I shared with her the power of God to bring healing and salvation. Kathy took me into the room to pray for little Tommy. He was one of the most precious little guys I ever saw. In spite of his dire condition he remained cheerful and happy. As time went on I became very close to that little boy. I bought him books and read to him and brought him toys and played with him. His conditioned worsened and I prayed all the harder for a miracle of healing. I grew to love Tommy so much that I felt I could not stand it if something happened to this little angel from above. He brought joy to the hearts of everybody that knew him.

Kathy introduced me to her sister, Patricia. The young ladies had been involved with gangs and substance abuse. Both needed to be saved and delivered. I shared scriptures with them and taught them about Jesus. They opened their hearts like flowers and let the Son of God come inside. They were gloriously saved! Their husbands were not as open to the Lord. Kathy's husband, Johnny, was into gangs and crime and was not ready to change his lifestyle for a life as Christ's disciple. I shared with him about the Lord. I saw in Johnny a strong leader with a tender heart that beat inside a tough outer shell. He was much like Saul of Tarsus who had been helplessly chained with the devil's shackles. Looking into his soft eyes you could see a tormented soul. He was polite to me and appreciated me praying for his son, Tommy, but Johnny wasn't yet ready to turn his life over to God. He reminded me of the incident in the Bible when King Agrippa told the Apostle Paul, "Almost, you persuade me to become a Christian."

Patricia's husband, Manuel was a similar story. He was Johnny's partner in their lifestyle. I tried to witness to him about Jesus, too. He became very angry that I had led his wife to the Lord. He warned me not to tell her any more about the Bible. However, it was too late. She had already invited Christ into her heart and did not want to go back to her old way of life! I had given Bibles to the two women and was having studies with them every day.

Then our secretary's grandson died in spite of all my prayers. I couldn't understand how this could happen because I had prayed so much for him. At the same time little Tommy's condition worsened. I began to fast and pray. Finally, the Lord spoke to me and said, "Tommy will bring many souls into everlasting joy."

I rejoiced, believing with all my heart that Tommy was going to be healed and grow up to be a great minister of the Lord to bring multitudes to Christ! I told his parents, Kathy and Johnny, that I believed God was going to heal little Tommy and raise him up to be a minister of the Lord that would win many souls for Jesus.

Then my world fell apart. Little Tommy died. My faith was shaken. My heart was broken. I had become so close to Tommy that it felt like my own son had passed away. I couldn't stop weeping. Why had God allowed him to die after giving me assurance that he was going to live? I told God, "Look at all the gang members and people that would have come to Christ if you had have done a miracle and healed little Tommy. Then his dad, Johnny, would have accepted you, and his uncle, Manuel, would have gotten saved, and all their relatives would have turned to you."

I went into a state of grief and depression over the loss of my little precious friend.

Kathy asked me to speak at Tommy's funeral and share the gospel. One of her brothers warned me not to do so or something bad would happen to me if I came! I was terrified and told God, "I don't mind preaching the gospel to anybody, except I don't do gangs!"

The Lord showed me that he wanted me to go anyway so reluctantly I told Kathy that I would. The Bible says, "Perfect love casts out all fear."

I thought I had perfect love, but fear was still lurking around the corner. Terrified, I made arrangements for my assistant pastor to go with me and act as my bodyguard.

Before I preached at Tommy's service, the Lord told me that He had not promised that little Tommy would be healed. The Holy Spirit gave me a poem that said Tommy's death "would bring many souls into everlasting joy."

During prayer at the close of the service several people raised their hands for salvation. Later, my worst fears came true when one of Johnny's brothers-in-law attacked me! My assistant pastor pulled him off and saved my life. I wanted nothing more to do with gangs. However, I had grown to love my sisters in the Lord, Kathy and Patricia. I did not want to see them go back to the gang life and fall away from the Lord. Since they did not live near my church in Hemet, I tried to encourage them to get hooked up with Victory Outreach in Los Angeles. I had met Sonny Arguinzoni, the pastor of that church which had an outreach to gangs and people with alcohol and drug addictions. All I could do was pray for them. I also prayed desperately for their husbands. They were good men who had become enslaved by the devil and needed to be freed.

I knew if Jesus didn't set them free, prison or death would be the possible end result. With the dramatic changes happening in my life though, I lost track of them. I knew that only when I got to heaven would I ever know what happened to them.

The event with little Tommy's passing and the gang episode was the proverbial final straw that pushed me into a complete physical and emotional burnout. I could no longer function as a proper father or pastor. I left my church and family and went to Mexico for six months of recuperation. During my time there I helped my missionary brother and his wife in their ministry. At last I felt strong enough to return home.

When I returned to Hemet, the unthinkable happened. My wife and family had left me! I was so devastated that I prayed for God to just let me die. This was not supposed to happen. We were supposed to be married forever! I just could not believe our marriage was actually over, and I tried to move back into the house. It finally sunk in that our marriage was really over when she called the sheriff and had him physically remove me from the premises!

Now, in addition to the incredible pain of loneliness I was buried under a mountain of failures. I was stripped down to nothing. I had lost everything in life that meant anything to me. My wife, my family, my church, my money, and my possessions were all gone. All I had left in this world was the clothes on my back and an old beat-up pickup truck given to me out of pity by the lady whose husband I had prayed out of the coma.

My sorrow was so overwhelming that I thought this must be how Jesus felt agonizing in the Garden of Gethsemane. That sorrow eventually turned into bitterness, and I did the very thing that I should not have done. I started running down my wife to our kids and told them that she was to blame for our breakup. This was a mistake that hurt my children and ended up backfiring. It caused my kids to not want to be around me anymore. Instead, they wanted nothing to do with me and supported their mother.

All my childhood loneliness at Carrie Tingley Crippled Children's Hospital came back and rushed over me like terrible waves. The pain was so severe that I was sure I was going to die soon with a literal broken heart. I just could not go on living. I did not believe in suicide, but I pleaded over and over with the Lord to "Please, please, let me die."

Chapter Six

THE RECOVERY

I BECAME A WASTED human being, just waiting to die. I lost forty pounds and looked like a walking skeleton. Then my younger brother, whose wife had just left him, contacted me and begged me to move to Phoenix, Arizona, and live with him. He said that he was going to take a year off work and try to recover from his loss. He said he would feed and clothe me until I could get on my feet again.

I decided to take my brother up on his offer and moved into his apartment in Phoenix. I had no hopes of a recovery though. I was the worst basket case anyone could imagine. I still cried myself to sleep every night and was so despondent during the day that I was sure I would not make it through another night. Even with my brother by my side, the great dark clouds of loneliness engulfed me.

Then, in one night, God suddenly changed my sorrow into joy. I went to a singles' Christmas party at Phoenix First Assembly of God. There I met the most beautiful angel that I had ever seen in my life! Her name was Anita Casanova. She was a blonde Italian, gorgeous on the outside and the most beautiful person on the inside that I had ever known. She took this broken wreck of humanity and helped me to begin the slow process of healing and recovery. With our eventual marriage, she became the greatest gift God ever gave to me in this life! In addition to a new wife, the Lord brought with my new wife her three wonderful children, two girls and a boy.

Anita was a wonderful Christian lady that desired to serve God above all else. From childhood she dreamed of going to the mission field. A failed marriage had shattered her dreams also. Her favorite Bible verse was Proverbs 28:13: *"A man who refuses to admit his mistakes can never be successful. But if he confesses and forsakes them, he gets another chance"*

I confessed to God that it was my sins that brought the destruction into my first marriage and family. Now I repented and wanted to "get another chance."

Anita believed God was giving her a second chance and she wanted us to go be missionaries someplace where others did not want to go. We received a call from a man that had been an elder for a time in the church where I was pastor in Lordsburg, New Mexico. He asked if we would consider coming to Douglas, Arizona, on the Mexican border and start a church there. Douglas was called the "armpit of Arizona." It was a scary border town, the hub of drug smuggling and the illegals' favorite gateway to America.

It was also seemingly impossible to get a house financed by the bank. I was very discouraged but Anita had incredible faith. Although we were turned down for a home loan twelve times, she refused to give up.

We survived solely on my wife's faith, because I was "O ye of little faith." On the thirteenth attempt, a bank impressed by Anita's tenacity and perseverance finally granted the loan for our first house together!

Chapter Seven

THE MIRACLES

IN THE BEGINNING it was rough. We were by ourselves with no family or friends. We had left our home, brothers and sisters, mothers and fathers, children and all our property in order to share the Good News of Jesus where others would not go. Many times we didn't even know how we were going to continue eating. However, we made a commitment to tithe ten percent of our income to God and set aside another ten percent for savings even if we had only beans to eat!

I would read the Bible out loud to God from Mark 10:29-30 in order to remind Him that He said: "Let me assure you that no one has ever given up anything—home, brothers, sisters, mother, father, children, or property—for love of me and to tell others the Good News who won't be given back, a hundred times over, homes, brothers, sisters, mothers, children, and land—with persecutions. All these will be his here on earth, and in the world to come he shall have eternal life."

It wasn't long until God began to answer His promise. One by one, sisters, brothers, children, family, and friends began to move down to Douglas in order to help us with God's outreach on the border.

The famous evangelist, Oral Roberts, started a savings program for young preachers by setting aside one million dollars to help young charismatic ministers. There were a few hundred of us that participated in the program that matched Oral Roberts's funds monthly in a mutual fund savings account. The idea was to encourage poorer young ministers to start saving. We barely had enough to cover our basic living expenses, but we sacrificed each month to put in as much as possible to get the matching funds. This lasted a few years before it ran out, but God blessed us immeasurably with this head start in our second chance at life! His son, Richard Roberts, also sent medical teams, eyeglasses, and hospital equipment to assist us in reaching the impoverished on the Mexican side of the border. We held free medical and vision clinics. Hundreds came and we provided free medicine, glasses, and Bibles. We prayed for each one, and many miracles took place. People of all ages were healed of various diseases, and some who were totally blind had their eyesight restored! Those who were not healed we fitted with eyeglasses for their individual prescription so they could see again. There were great lines and hundreds were helped. We truly felt like the hands of Jesus reaching out to the needy.

Because of the free clinics we found great favor with the Mexican government, and they donated to us land in Naco, Mexico, to build an orphanage. Businessmen from the United States sent materials and laborers to help us construct the orphanage that would be named Hogar De Los Niños.

Then another great miracle took place when a mobile home community donated to us land and buildings for our church and Christian school! We also found favor with the United States Federal Government when the Justice Department approved us to get visas for Mexican children to cross the border and attend our school. Many young people accepted Jesus as their Savior, and their lives were forever changed. God fulfilled another part of my vision, "You will reach souls in Mexico."

Anita's two daughters, their husbands, and Anita's sister and brother-in-law all moved down to Douglas to work in our church and teach in the Christian school.

It wasn't long until even some children from China heard about our school and came for an education. One Chinese brother and sister in our school came to live with us as our own children. Their parents divorced, and the mother moved to Japan. We felt sorry for them and kept them for several years raising them like our own kids. They were of the Buddhist faith.

One day they had a falling out with one of their Chinese friends who also attended our school. The friend no longer wanted to stay because of the ill feelings and moved away to live with relatives in San Francisco. Shortly after the breakup of their friendship we had to make a trip to Southern California, and our Chinese kids had to go with us. They were afraid to make the trip because they thought we could possibly run into their Chinese friend-turned-enemy that moved to San Francisco. We explained how big California was and that it would be impossible for us to run into somebody living in Northern California if we just went to Ontario, in Southern California. Finally, I told them that if we did run into their enemy it would have to be the miraculous hand of Jesus trying to reconcile them. Our Chinese daughter said, "If such a thing were to happen, I would really have to believe in your Jesus."

We made the trip to Ontario, California with our Chinese kids, and stopped at the big shopping center mall. As we opened the door to enter the mall, there was their former friend, now enemy, coming out of the mall at the same time! They both screamed in shock and our Chinese daughter threw her arms around her former friend and sobbed uncontrollably. All was forgiven between them, and she had to admit that only Jesus could have done such an unbelievable miracle as to bring two souls together from hundreds of miles apart to meet at a designated spot in time and space! This was one of the greatest miracles any of us had ever heard about in our whole lives! Her brother stood dumbfounded unable to speak at all. Needless to say, that event caused both of our Chinese kids to become believers.

God opened doors for us to start a Bible college to train ministers in neighboring Sierra Vista, Arizona. A church there opened their doors to house our college. We were finding favor with God and man.

The miracles did not stop. People began to donate land and property to us, and many of our friends and family were now involved in this incredible ministry. Truly, God was fulfilling the exact words of His promise to us in Mark 10.

One of our Christian worker's sons, Curtis, and daughter-in-law, Tanja, were living in California at the time. The young couple was doing drugs and alcohol, and had separated. Tanja decided to move in with her mother-in-law and father-in-law where they were ministering with us in Douglas. The young woman came to Christ and was radically saved. After six months, Curtis decided he wanted to try to get their marriage back on track, so he moved to Douglas also. Curtis didn't turn his life over to the Lord right away, so Tanja would come to church without him. She would cry and cry at the altar, praying for a child. She said the doctors had said they could not have children, but she believed God to give her kids. I prayed with her. Then one night I received a call from a Christian lady in Mexico asking if I knew of anyone that would like a baby. I called Tanja and told her that a Mexican baby was available and maybe this was God's way of answering her prayer. She agreed and took the child. It had been abused and was severely brain-damaged. His entire life would be spent like a happy little infant. They didn't care. The couple took the babe and loved it just the same as if it were normal. They even named him Curtis, Jr. I felt so sorry for them that I poured my heart out to God, pleading with Him to give them some healthy children. God answered my prayers by sending two more babies, Daniel and Christian, for them to adopt. Jesus revealed himself to Curtis, and he came to Christ as well. Their marriage was restored. They were delivered from the devil's bondage and were now a completed happy family.

Many years later, great sadness came upon this family. Tanja and her mother-in-law both died within a short time of each other. With overwhelming grief at the loss of his wife and mother, Curtis was left to raise their sons alone. Anita and I introduced our eldest daughter, Debi, to him and soon they got married. Curtis's great time of sorrow was washed away, and a new life of happiness has begun. Miracle of miracles—now the two boys that I had prayed into that family so many years ago are now my own precious grandsons! Who would ever believe that when I was praying for sons for Curtis and Tanja, I was praying for two wonderful grandsons for Anita and me! I never cease to be amazed at all the miracles God has done in our lives!

Chapter Eight
THE TRANSITION

One thing God corrected in my life by moving to Douglas, Arizona, was the importance of learning to budget our money. I took courses in financial planning because I never wanted again to go through the terrible monetary crashes that I had experienced a number of times during my life. God used the extreme pain from these episodes to turn me into a good fiscal manager.

During the summers when our Christian school was out, Anita and I would travel to other states in our motor home. My wife was very gifted in real estate, and God directed us to incredible house bargains in Oregon and California. We were able to use these homes as rentals generating more income for us and the ministry. We were prospering in every way imaginable. God was using us to bring many souls into the Kingdom through the ministries He had led us into and was blessing us financially beyond anything we could have imagined.

However, God was ready to make a transition in our lives. Like a mother bird, when things are too comfy in the nest, she kicks her chicks out to find their way in the world. God allowed our secure nest to fall apart. The State of Arizona allowed several free government-financed charter schools to open in Douglas. The parents in Mexico realized that their children could be given a private school type of education without having to pay hundreds of dollars per month at our Christian school. Most of our students fled to the charter schools to save their money. We knew that financially we could not keep the Christian school operating. This was a sign from God that He wanted to move us into a new ministry.

We turned the leadership of the orphanage over to a minister who was a Mexican national working in Naco, Mexico. The Bible college in Sierra Vista, Arizona, closed. Our assistant pastor became the minister of the church, and we allowed the remnant of our Christian school to be operated by the Hispanic school principal and his wife.

Another former assistant pastor and his wife were from England. Their son was the pastor of a church in the U.K., and he invited us to come and preach at the church he pastored. He said that he could get us booked in Ireland and the United Kingdom for meetings. I got very excited remembering what God had told me as a youth: "You will reach souls in the land of your mother's ancestors, Ireland, and you will reach souls in the land of your father's ancestors, England."

At the time, problems arose with our Chinese kids that prevented us from making the trip to the U.K. Because of an unfortunate incident, our Chinese children were deported and not allowed to return to the United States. However, there was no problem for them to get visas to stay in Canada.

I also recalled that when God called me into the ministry as a young man, He said that I would "reach souls in Canada."

I now became convinced that God was leading us to move to Vancouver, Canada. I eventually convinced my wife, Anita, to go along with the plan. We loved our Chinese kids dearly and felt that we had a responsibility to continue raising them. We got our visas, packed up our motor home with all our important belongings, and headed north to a new adventure with God.

On the way we decided to stop in and visit my sister and her husband in Medford, Oregon. He was an evangelist and prophet of God. He immediately told us that it was not God's will for us to move to Canada. I protested and even got angry with him for trying to stop us from moving to Vancouver. He said he had prayed a lot about it and God showed him that it was not the Lord's will for us to move to Canada. He then asked, "John, how long did you pray about this?"

I felt frustrated when I thought about it. I guessed we hadn't really prayed about it. We just assumed it was the Lord's will. I prayed and reluctantly agreed with my brother-in-law. The timing was not right for us to make a move into Canada. We turned the motor home around and returned to Douglas, Arizona.

All of our ministries along the border began falling apart. Words cannot describe my despondency. I felt confused not knowing what I had done wrong. I had tried so hard to find God's perfect will for our lives and it seemed there was no clear direction. I had failed fulfilling God's vision to reach souls in Israel, England, Ireland, and now even Canada.

All I could do was to wait on the Lord. When God closes a door He opens another. However, sometimes it doesn't happen on our timetable, and we get very frustrated.

Eventually God laid on my heart to open charter schools in Phoenix, Arizona. Ironically, these were the very type of schools that had destroyed our ministry in Douglas! God works in strange ways. We then sold all the property and possessions that we could quickly liquidate and moved to Phoenix.

The startup costs to begin a charter school were enormous, and we didn't begin to have enough money. We told the Lord that if this really was His will, He would have to provide. The Holy Spirit soon gave me ideas. We sold our houses in California and Oregon to raise cash and were able to get relatives to help supply money and come in as partners in developing the schools. God blessed us wonderfully! Our niece, Melissa, came in early on to help us administer two schools in the Phoenix area, and our daughter, Debi, became a Special Education teacher to assist us there. Another of our daughters, Connie, helped us administer a school in Prescott Valley, Arizona, where she lived. Eventually much of our family that had worked with us on the Mexican border, as well as other church members and friends, moved to Phoenix just to teach and work with us in the charter schools.

During the first couple of years we were able to reach many children for Christ through weekly chapel services and afterschool programs conducted by our youth minister. Local and state governments finally forced us to stop the ministries held on school property. At the same time, my precious wife, Anita was experiencing a worsening heart condition. This caused me great concern. Next to Jesus, she was the most important thing in my life.

We were nearing the age when most people retire, so we purchased a home in Oregon on the coast. It would be ideal for summer vacations and school breaks, and then could serve as a retirement home when the time came.

One day, shortly after acquiring the Oregon house, I heard a crash in the bedroom. It was my beloved Anita. She collapsed from a speeding heartbeat and hit the dresser on her way down! I picked her up and got her in the car and started driving as fast as I could to the hospital. On the way there her heart totally stopped and she fell against me. I screamed out, "Anita! Don't you dare die on me! God, please don't let her die!"

I pulled the car to the curb and ran around and tried to pull her out and resuscitate her when all of a sudden she woke up and asked, "What are you doing?"

Praise God! He gave Anita her life back! I finally got her to the hospital where they stabilized her and had us rush in an ambulance to St. Vincent's Hospital in Portland, Oregon. Before they could do emergency surgery to save her life she flatlined! Again, sobbing, I cried out to God, "Please! Please, let her live! If you will save her life I will retire and spend the rest of my days ministering to her. She is the greatest gift that you ever gave me in this life; please don't take that gift away!"

The doctors shocked her heart six times with the electric paddles, but to no avail. Finally, on the seventh attempt, the screen bleeped and her heart started beating again! I cried with relief, and tears of joy ran down my face!

Anita was taken into surgery and the operation was successful! Praise God for His goodness and mercy to us! Her recuperation was slow and she had to be hospitalized a couple more times before she had a full recovery.

Chapter Nine

THE REVELATION

I KEPT MY WORD to God and immediately retired after God brought my precious Anita back to me. My life slowed to a snail's pace compared to what the previous sixty-five years had been. We did cruises, traveled around America, and visited our children, grandchildren, and great-grandchildren that were spread over the country.

However, the passion for winning souls never left me. We developed friendships at our home in Oregon and led people to Christ. We were led to help pastors and missionaries in need with the money God had given to us. Some of those we brought to our home in Oregon for a much-needed rest. I became an elder in an Oregon church helping with the teaching and counseling. We also assisted them in keeping their Christian school open.

Still, I felt like I had failed God in the mission He had called me to do. And now it was too late. I was approaching seventy years of age with many places still remaining to reach souls. I felt like I had not done enough for God who did everything for me. It seemed to me that one thing after another kept blocking the places where I thought the Holy Spirit was directing me. Wouldn't it be great if we could just pull back the veil and see what we have done that has counted for eternity?

On my seventieth birthday, Anita's side of the family threw a big celebration for my birthday. My son flew all the way from the East Coast to surprise me with a visit, and our niece, to whom I had turned over the running of the charter schools, flew out to my Oregon home and woke me up with balloons, posters and the singing of "Happy Seventieth Birthday."

I reflected on the seventy years the Lord had shown his goodness to me. God had given me a second chance at life. He blessed me with Anita, the most wonderful wife that any man could ever have! To top it off, her children accepted and loved me just like their own father. Together, we had obeyed Christ's admonition about "feeding my lambs." The little orphans in Sonora, Mexico, now had a nice Christian facility to help them get a good start in life. The charter schools that we had started were continually growing with more young people added every year. Oh, how Jesus had shown His love for me. However, it seemed that after seventy years, I could have done much more for our Lord.

I looked back on my life to see how it measured up to other people's lives. I know better than to compare my life with others, but sometimes we fall into that trap. I think now I must have lived my life with delusions of grandeur. I always believed I was going to be somebody great… like a Billy Graham or an Oral Roberts, reaching great multitudes for Christ, instead of being just an ordinary man. When a person has ideas about what he wants to do with his life rather than knowing exactly what God wants him to do, it can leave disappointments from not reaching one's self-appointed goals. The Bible speaks of three basic sins—the lust of the flesh, the lust of the eyes, and the pride of life (1 John 1:16). We all like to be noticed and want to feel important. Some of us are not satisfied with just being ordinary. I had definitely fallen into the deadly sin of the pride of life.

After seventy years of tramping down the path of life, the few baubles, the property, and the money I had acquired seemed unimportant now. These were all items that in the eternal scheme of things mean nothing. This stuff brings no lasting joy and will all pass away with this life.

As my mind wandered back over these seventy years I realized that my happiest moments were winning souls to Christ—not chasing worthless stuff. I remember as a boy that I couldn't wait to turn twenty-one. But now I was not in a hurry to turn seventy! Perhaps I didn't try hard enough to go to all the places the Lord showed me I would reach in that boyhood vision. I never made it to Canada, England, Ireland, or Israel. And now I felt like too many years had slipped by and I had missed fulfilling God's complete plan for my life.

That big "7-0" birthday somehow triggered a sense of incompleteness in God's plan for my life. I think that my lack of understanding about why God had allowed certain things to happen left me with many unanswered questions. "Why were my petitions for deliverance not strong enough to break the bondage of alcohol and tobacco for Sammy Davis, Jr.? Why were my prayers of faith not effectual enough to bring healing to my precious friend, "Little Tommy"? Why were my words not powerful enough to convince Tommy's dad, Johnny, to become a Christian? Why was my trust in God not strong enough to overcome my fear of gangs? Why was my ability as a pastor not good enough to faithfully look after my disciples, like Tommy's mom and aunt? Why were my skills as a father and husband not great enough to keep my family together? Why was I not able to go to all the places I thought the Lord had sent me? Why does God not reveal these answers to me now?

I wept and cried out, "Oh, Lord, please don't keep it a secret from me. I am sure we will know everything in Heaven, but is there any way You can answer any of my questions right now?"

Then almost immediately I received a long distance phone call from a pastor. He said, "John, are you still alive?"

I laughed and said, "I believe so."

He then told me that God laid on his heart an urgency to locate and talk to me. He was one of the young men that I had talked into attending the Bible college I started in Sierra Vista, Arizona. He went on to relate how I helped him to graduate from our Bible seminary and enter the ministry. He shared how I assisted him in pioneering a church and helped him start a Christian school. He said that all the people he had led to the Lord over these many years were my fruit. He went on to relate how that God had instructed him to let me know that my labor in the Lord was not in vain. He continued, "Many of the people saved in this ministry went on to reach more souls in other places, and you, Pastor John, will keep on reaching souls in this way until Jesus returns!"

After that phone call I broke down and cried tears of joy! "Wow! God really does love me and hears my cries!"

Then the Lord showed me from that phone call that when God revealed His plan for my life as a teenage boy, it was not a command for me to personally go to every place on earth, but that I would "reach souls" around the world through others. That was a great revelation to me and instantly a tremendous weight was lifted that had gotten heavier and heavier over my lifetime! God showed me then and there that He has a master plan for reaching souls, and each of us is but one small cog in the link of His great mission machine to seek and to save the lost. I did not have to be a super-evangelist or a famous person. Wow! That is terrific, especially since I didn't make it!

I had thought I would have to wait until I got to heaven to see if anything I had ever done bore fruit.

If that was not enough, God then put the icing on my seventieth birthday cake with a forwarded letter that arrived at my present residence. It was from Little Tommy's father, who I had tried to lead to Christ in 1984. It read:

Dear John Atkinson,

My name is Johnny Heredia and my wife's name is Kathy. In April of 1984 our son Tommy was diagnosed with neuroblastoma (cancer) and was admitted to UCLA Medical Center in Los Angeles. He went to be with the Lord in July of that same year.

During and prior to my son becoming sick, I was a twenty-two-year-old, drug-addicted, ex-gang member and generally hurting person, looking for an escape from life. My wife Kathy was also bound to alcohol and had been raised in the gang lifestyle. Our whole family was on a definite path to destruction. But God somehow brought hope into our lives during this tragic time.

A man named John Atkinson (hopefully this is you!) from Hemet, California, ministered to my wife and her sister in the hospital lobby. After hearing the message of hope, my wife and her sister both received the Lord, though I did not. After my son passed away, you attended and spoke at my son's funeral, and your daughter sang "I want to stay on the mountaintop fellowshipping with the Lord." I have always remembered that and have tried for years to find you and tell you what became of us.

Well, the other day while going thru my wife's ninety-eight-year-old grandmother's things (after she died), we found a letter written to "Tommy," my son, by John Atkinson of Mountain View Christian Center in Hemet, California. This letter was apparently written after my son died and was given to my wife, but somehow ended up with her grandmother's belongings. It said much, but one verse read "Tommy we have identified what your purpose in life was, and that is to lead your family to God..."

John, I want to let you know your words in that letter were prophetic, and your labor in the Lord has not been in vain, for you have touched lives you have not known of! In 1984 you led my wife and her sister to the Lord, while my brother-in-law (and partner-in-crime) followed shortly afterward. Then, after a year of misery, pain, and heart-ache, and a lot of people's prayers, I surrendered and gave my heart to Jesus in 1985 and went to the Victory Outreach Men's Ranch in Helendale, California, where I was set free from my addictions.

In 1990 my wife and I were sent to Seattle, Washington, to begin Victory Outreach Seattle (www.voseattle.org) where we pastor a thriving church today. All of my children, including four sons (three born after Tommy) and one daughter, are serving God. We have been blessed with six grandsons and one granddaughter. Almost all of my grandsons and one nephew are either named Thomas or have their middle name Thomas after their brother or cousin who led the way.

John, it gets better: Today my brother-in-law and his wife, Manuel and Patricia Cervantez, who you led to the Lord, are pastoring a Victory Outreach Church in Vancouver, Canada. My other brother-in-law (who you may remember) tried to attack either you or the other pastor. My pastor, Mitchell Peterson of Victory Outreach, who attended the after-funeral get-together (where there was much drinking) is now pastoring a Victory Outreach Church with his wife in Surrey, Canada. A couple who attended the funeral and were bound to drugs and prison life, eventually got saved and are pastoring a Victory Outreach Church in Dublin, Ireland. All of our family, fathers, mothers, cousins, nieces, nephews, and many of our friends are now saved and serving God!

It gets better: From our church we have discipled couples and sent them to several different cities, including Vancouver, Canada; Tacoma, Washington; Tri-Cities, Washington; Yakima, Washington; and Memphis, Tennessee. We oversee ten churches in the northwest region. We were also able to reach a man and his wife early in our ministry who was living in an alley bound to alcohol; today that man pastors in Jerusalem, Israel. From the church in Dublin, there are five more churches in Ireland and the U.K.

And even more good news: Two of my nieces are pastor's wives, my son is a regional G.A.N.G. (God's Anointed Now Generation) overseer. Two of my nephews are youth leaders in their churches; another niece runs a women's recovery home. A cousin is a pastor's wife and runs a women's shelter. My mother-in-law, who was a devout Catholic, has been saved along with her husband for the last twenty years, my brother plays on the worship team, and my father went to be with the Lord in 2010, but not before accepting Jesus into his heart. And there are more I don't have time to mention…

John, I write this letter to thank you for planting that seed so many years ago. I don't know what kinds of battles life has brought you, but know that your labor in the Lord has not been in vain!

I hope with all my heart that this letter reaches you and that you are the John Atkinson who ministered to my family twenty-eight years ago. Our church website is www.voseattle.org – and our address is 10821 1st Avenue, South Seattle, WA 98168.

May God Bless,

Pastor Johnny, C. Heredia,
Victory Outreach Seattle

When I read the letter from Johnny Heredia I cried so profusely that I couldn't even see the pages for a long time. So much joy overwhelmed me that I thought surely I would die from rejoicing! Then I called Johnny on the phone and continued to rejoice when I heard his voice. He couldn't talk long because he was in the hospital ministering to somebody just like I did with him twenty-eight years before!

Then joy came like waves over us when Anita and I visited the Victory Outreach of Seattle, Washington. Johnny and Kathy asked me to preach the sermon to a large packed-out church. Then after the service a line of people came up, and some of them told me of how they were gang members that came to little Tommy's funeral twenty-eight years before and heard me share the gospel! Unknown to me, they had found Jesus and left the Los Angeles gangs to follow Johnny and Kathy Heredia to Seattle and work with them in the church there. We met ones that operated men's ministry houses and women's ministry houses for recovering addicts, alcoholics, and gang members. They all had such wonderful testimonies to share. I thought that this must be the way it will be when we get to heaven!

We will then have an eternity to share with each other all the victories we experienced through Jesus our Lord. We will then get to see all the souls that each of us was responsible for bringing to Christ. We have no idea now about how many people will be in heaven because of our walk on this earth. Only eternity will show us the results.

While in this life, we all have to walk by faith, believing that our "labor for the Lord is not in vain," but seldom seeing the impact that our lives have made on others. Sometimes not knowing causes great discouragement and feelings of futility. Coupled with all our sins as human beings, it is so easy to think that we really aren't that valuable to God and His great plan; in fact we believe at times that we have actually messed up God's master plan. Rarely in this world does God ever reveal to us the true impact we have had on another person's life.

I now rejoice knowing that I fulfilled the calling God gave me so many years ago. I am forever grateful to God, that while I am still on this earth before I get to Heaven, He gave me just a glimpse of some of the lives that I have touched!

ABOUT THE AUTHOR

JOHN ATKINSON RECEIVED his Doctorate in Theology from School of Bible Theology in San Jacinto, California, while in his mid forties. After a lifetime as a pastor, evangelizing, and starting schools, he retired with his wife, Anita, and resides on the Oregon coast. They have seven children, nineteen grandchildren, and six great-grandchildren. John is still the volunteer superintendent of the Prescott Valley Schools in Arizona, as well as helps in a number of churches and ministries as an elder, pastor emeritus and board member. He can be reached at jatkinson@cox.net.